CW00689981

MANIFESTOS FOR THE 21ST CENTURY

SERIES EDITORS: URSULA OWEN AND JUDITH VIDAL-HALL

Free expression is as high on the agenda as it has ever been, though not always for the happiest of reasons. Here, distinguished writers address the issue of censorship in a complex and fragile world where people with widely different cultural habits and beliefs are living in close proximity, where offence is easily taken, and where words, images and behaviour are coming under the closest scrutiny. These books will surprise, clarify and provoke in equal measure.

Index on Censorship is the only international magazine promoting and protecting free expression. A haven for the censored and silenced, it has built an impressive track record since it was founded 35 years ago, publishing some of the finest writers, sharpest analysts and foremost thinkers in the world. In this series with Seagull Books, the focus will be on questions of rights, liberties, tolerance, silencing, censorship and dissent.

OFFENCE

the muslim case

KAMILA SHAMSIE

Seagull
BOOKS

LONDON NEW YORK CALCUTTA

Seagull Books 2009

© Kamila Shamsie 2009

ISBN-13   978 1 90649 703 3

British Library Cataloguing-in-Publication Data
A catalogue record for this book is available
from the British Library

Typeset and designed by Seagull Books, Calcutta, India
Printed in Calcutta at Rockwel Offset

CONTENTS

There are moments in history when particular words seem to exert a magnetic field, drawing other words to them. In the early years of our present century, that magnetic field can be found around the word 'Islam', pulling in a host of words of which the most thickly clustered is 'Terror' and, hard on its heels, the word 'Offence'.

Living as I now do in London, where Muslims are a minority, though a significant one, it seems I can never go very far without running into the spectre of the Offended

Muslim. I ran into that spectre when asked to write this piece: two friends, independently of each other and neither of them Muslim, told me to 'be careful'. And as they said the words I saw that spectre rise up before their eyes. The more time I spend reading or hearing about this spectre from those who don't live in the Muslim world, the more I am struck by the fact that, far more often than not, the figure of the Offended Muslim is merely partial.

By 'partial' I mean if you utter the words 'Islam' and 'Offence' together, much of the non-Muslim world will doubtless think, 'Danish cartoons . . . *The Satanic Verses* . . . teddy bears named Muhammad . . . children's stories with pigs as protagonists . . . women in skimpy clothes . . . bars and nightclubs . . .' In other words, Offence is what happens when Muslims encounter the West.

The Offended Muslim is regarded as an anti-Western construct and, as such, falls quite readily into the rhetoric of a 'Clash of Civilizations' between Islam and the West.

And yet, as a Muslim woman who was raised in the Islamic Republic of Pakistan and continues to spend a fair amount of time there, I know that the name of Islam is invoked over a range of perceived offences, most of them entirely without reference to the non-Muslim world. These offences include cricket songs that predict victory without accounting for Allah's will, female heads of state, boys playing football. They also include suicide bombings, forced marriages and excessive reverence (running the risk of deification) towards the Prophet Muhammad. And, of course, every sect within Islam finds reason to be offended by every other sect.

Offence and Islam, then, is a wide-ranging issue—I would go so far as to argue that it is primarily an intra-Muslim affair and only secondarily concerned with the non-Muslim world. And the manner in which offence is expressed varies almost as substantially as the causes of offence—from violent acts to tears shed in private, from parliamentary decrees to protest poetry.

One could ask, 'Why does Islam give so much occasion for Offence?' but any scrutiny of the word 'sacred' and any glance at history answers the question. It is not merely Islam, but religions worldwide that carry with them demands for reverence and adherence to religious laws. Since this latter requirement is not necessary for 'non-believers', there are fewer incidences of Offence between religions than within a religion. And, of course, the world's particular interest in Islam and Offence does not gather around Muslims who shed private tears or write protest poetry when their religious sensibilities are offended, but around those Muslims who articulate Offendedness in the form of violence and threats of violence. So the really pressing question is: why has the Violently Offended Muslim become such a prominent figure? There are those who argue that Islam lends itself to violence, but this point of view entirely ignores the fact that the entwining of Islam, Violence and Offence has not existed in an unbroken thread through the centuries, but has become significant in very recent history.

To understand this entwining it is necessary to step away from the partial viewpoint that regards Offence through an 'Islam vs the West' prism. We cannot hope to understand any part of the diffuse and diverse Muslim world if we fail to take into account the internal history of different sects, groups and nations that has allowed the hardliners to grow in strength and put their stamp on the most visible global face of Islam. So rather than viewing the matter of Offence as one of Muslims vs the West, it might cast some light if we recast it as hard-liners vs anti-hardliners, a varied group that includes moderate Muslims, secularist Muslims, non-Muslims, etc: in short, those who, for varying reasons, oppose the ascendancy of the hardliners. This is not to imply the anti-hardliners band together or see themselves as a unity but, rather, to identify them in opposition to those who call for violence in the name of religion.

I remember quite clearly the first time the transnational figure of the Offended Muslim acquired global significance. It was 1989: I was a teenager in Karachi with dreams of one day being a writer and a book called *The Satanic Verses* became the biggest news story of the day. With the exception of Turkey, every Muslim-majority nation—as well as several with large Muslim minorities—banned the novel on the grounds of its offensiveness to Islam.

The widespread banning of the novel certainly seemed to point to the fact that, in the confrontation between 'freedom of expression' and 'due respect for religion', an overwhelming majority of Muslims would come down in favour of the latter. But this confrontation and its outcome are not peculiar to Islam: in any religion where the word 'blasphemy' exists, there is a point beyond which freedom of expression becomes transgression. The confrontation and its outcome are far less significant than the particular nature of the response to transgression. The fact that so many believing Muslims were offended by *The Satanic Verses*—or, rather, by what they were told was written about Muhammad in the book—can pass almost without comment; what do require more detailed analysis are the calls for violence, and the violence itself, that followed.

It is easy to see why anyone from the outside viewing the protests, the banning of the book, the calls for violence from Muslims in different parts of the world, would think they were viewing a Monolith of the Offended Muslim ranged against the Freedoms of the West. But from where I was sitting, in Karachi, I remember the one question that had me transfixed: why are the British burning copies of this book? Even at 16 I could entirely understand the reasons for reactions in Pakistan being what they were, but what was going on in Britain? It was entirely baffling. Years later, I saw the bafflement of my 16-year-old self reflected in my Pakistani compatriots when I returned to Karachi from London after the 7/7 bombings on the London Underground in 2005 to questions of, 'What's going on with these British Muslims? What does Britain do to these people?' While the British press was stressing the Muslimness of the bombers, Pakistanis saw the root cause in nation. 'Sure, we have our own

suicide bombers, but at least we know,
broadly speaking, who they are, where they
come from and why they're doing it,' more
than one Pakistani said to me. 'These boys
from Yorkshire just don't make sense.'

The Bradford book-burners didn't
make sense to me either because the fact
that someone is Muslim has never been in
itself an indicator or explanation of any-
thing. I was living in a country that was 98
per cent Muslim which made for great het-
erogeneity, ranging from militant jihadis to
whirling dervishes and to don't-fast, don't-
pray, don't-abstain-from-alcohol-or-premar-
ital-sex but-of-course-I'm-a-Believer
Muslims. 'Muslim' was a word that con-
tained within it so many colours that it was
itself without hue. The only way to prevent
it from appearing as a blinding whiteness,
revealing nothing, was to place it against
some kind of defining context. The most
obvious of these contexts, the one that most

effectively allowed the different colours to separate and stand in opposition to or overlap each other, was—is—nation.

I've spent enough time now in England to begin to understand something about the Bradford book burnings. But not enough: I cannot go beyond a general discussion of the rage of second-generation Asian migrants in self-enclosed communities to discuss the particulars of what happened in Bradford. It is when I turn my eye to Pakistan, the country whose history and politics and social life I know best, that I am able most clearly to understand all the reactions to offence. What I see is often frustrating, horrifying, maddening—but never baffling. The only thing that is baffling is expert commentators from outside the Muslim world who continue to quote the Quran and Hadith (sayings of the Prophet) in explanation of Muslim reactions to offence rather than recognizing the plurality of interpretation within the Islamic tradition and asking, more pertinently: why, at a precise collision of history and geography, should certain forms of interpretations be privileged over others, or gain ascendance in political, though not necessarily numerical, terms, often in contravention of historical trends in that region? And why do the most damaging forms of interpretation currently co-exist at so many points of geographic and historic collision?

Anyone who doubts that there are widely varying forms of interpretation within Islam has clearly never watched *Aalim Online*, a popular television show in Pakistan where scholars from different sects debate religious questions. All the scholars proffer Quranic verses and Hadith in defence of their own positions and often end up with radically contrasting views. And yes, the position on the punishment for blasphemy and the authority necessary to make

judgements about blasphemy does vary
considerably among scholars.

THE PAKISTAN STORY

In the two decades since the publication of
The Satanic Verses, there have been repeated
instances when Muslims in different parts
of the world have protested the same inci-
dents, yet nothing has changed my view:
that in order to understand what's going
on, it is essential to understand the national
politics and history of those countries
whose citizens are involved in the protests.
Why, for instance, do second-generation
Muslim migrants in the UK respond differ-
ently to Religious Offence from second-
generation Muslim migrants in the US?
Why do the countries of South Asia feature
so much more prominently in these protests
than the countries of West Africa?

I shall confine myself here to a particular nation, Pakistan, using it as a case study to demonstrate the interplay of national politics and religious ideology. Specifically: in what political moments have offences to Islam lead to protests, and what form have those protests taken? Who or what has been targeted by hardliners as Offensive to Islam? What has the role of hardliners been within the state, and how has the nature of hardliners changed over the decades? More generally, I hope to show how successive decisions by the state have led to the present condition in which religion and violence are entwined to an unprecedented extent. I'm using the word 'hardliner' as a catch-all phrase for different groups in different times, united only by the fact that their interpretations of Islam give fuel to the Violently Offended Muslim by stressing violent punishment over opportunities for repentance, and by their sidelining of courts of law in decisions about innocence and guilt.

It should become apparent that my discussion of the ascendancy of the hardliners in Pakistan ties in to the ascendancy of the hardliners in other parts of the world. In some cases, there will be parallels with other postcolonial nations; in others, Pakistani migrants moving to non-Muslim nations will continue to look to Pakistan for spiritual guidance; in yet others, the history of Pakistan intersects with the history of other nations.

Hardline Islam strengthened within Pakistan—where it remained a regional affair for a while, its effects felt in Pakistan, Afghanistan, India—before it became of concern to the West. We have to go back to the origins of the hardliners' ascent, to a period before the phrase 'Clash of Civilizations', and to the history of Offence between different sects of Islam in order to make sense of Muslim reactions to cartoons, novels, teddy bears and fairytale pigs.

Moreover, in this world where the 'Clash of Civilizations' is becoming a self-fulfilling prophecy, we have to understand that Muslims are not a monolith that can be placed on one side of a divide, lobbing grenades at the West but, rather, that the fault-lines within Islam are so deep that the illusion of a united *ummah* (community of the faithful) is no more than an illusion, often perpetrated by lazy or uninformed reporting that is only interested in portraying one side of a story.

There are two inter-related strands in my case study: the hardliners' political ascent, and the relationship between Islam and Christendom/the West.

There is an immediate roadblock, of course, in wanting to discuss the specific case of Pakistan: where to begin? In 1947, with the creation of Pakistan? Earlier, with the demands for Pakistan? Earlier still, with Muslims in colonial India? Or even earlier,

with Mughal rule in India? The first two
options are hard to discuss without some
mention of the latter two, but I'll confess to
some queasiness about choosing the latter
and thus giving in to the official version of
history in Pakistan which says the history of
the nation is, pre-1947, synonymous with
the history of Muslims in India. On one
hand, such a view presupposes that the history of Muslims in India can be separated
from the history of India; on the other, it
dismisses non-Muslim-related historical
events that took place within the geograph-
ically bounded space that forms Pakistan.
But it is within this conflict that part of the
nature of Pakistan's particular grappling
with religion arises. Because the nation
chooses the history of Muslims within the
subcontinent over the history of territorial
Pakistan, it creates a particular notion of
identity as wrapped up with religion in a
manner quite distinct from notions of iden-

tity in, for example, Indonesia, the nation
with the world's largest Muslim population.

But with the caveat that I'm not talking
about Pakistan's history per se, but about
the history of Pakistan as it relates to Islam
and Offence, I'm putting aside my queasiness. There must be an element of arbi-
trariness to any starting point of a topic
such as this, but, for reasons that should become clear, this discussion will start in the
decade 1857–67.

The starting date will be familiar: the
year of the Indian Mutiny or Revolt or Rebellion or War of Independence. Although
both Hindus and Muslims took part in that
anti-British rebellion, the rallying point was
the aged Mughal emperor, Bahadur Shah
Zafar. At his trial, after the rebellion was
quashed, the prosecutor alleged that it was
'to Musalman intrigues and Mahommedan
conspiracy we may mainly attribute the
dreadful calamities of 1857'.[1] It was a wide-

spread view among the British in part because of Zafar's 'leadership', but also because it tapped into an old narrative, one
larger than that of Britain or India: the narrative of Islam vs Christendom, a continuing force in the relationship of Islam and
the West, with the 'West' serving as merely
another word for 'Christendom'. Scholar
and activist Eqbal Ahmad points out that:

> The Islamic civilisation is the only one
> with which the territorial, religious and
> cultural boundaries of the West have
> fluctuated for fourteen centuries . . .
> This unique history of the West's en-
> counter with a non-Western civilisation
> undoubtedly left on both sides a her-
> itage of prejudice and resentment.[2]

My comments on the importance of un-
derstanding national events in no way deny
this narrative: the specific events within
India in 1857 provided both opportunity
and framework for the larger narrative to

re-assert itself, as it had done for centuries.
In addition, specific geo-political events,
such as the aftermath of 1857, shifted the
terms of engagement between the two sides
in this grand narrative. From Napoleon's
invasion of Egypt in 1798 to the trial of
Zafar, Western imperialism had laid rout to
Muslim rulers.

> For the first time in a long and eventful
> history Islamic civilisation began to be
> defined by reference to another . . . A
> people habituated to a history of suc-
> cess were reduced to serving another's
> history.[3]

This, then, was the situation in 1861
when the London publishers South, Elder
and Company produced the complete four
volume set of *The Life of Mahomet* by William
Muir, a British intelligence officer stationed
in India. Muir, firmly ensconced in the
Islam vs Christianity narrative, was in no
doubt that 'the sword of Mahomet and the

Quran are the most fatal enemies of Civilization, Liberty and Truth which the world has yet ever known.' Among the 'radical evils' arising from Islam was this:

> [A] barrier has been interposed against the reception of Christianity . . . Many a flourishing land in Africa and Asia which once rejoiced in the light and liberty of Christianity is now overspread by gross darkness and a stubborn barbarism.[4]

How's that for offensive to Muslim sensibilities? As the historian Ayesha Jalal notes of Muir's comments on Islam and the Prophet: 'There was enough ammunition here for a million Muslim mutinies.'[5] Her mention of 'mutinies' is well chosen: Muir was posted in Agra during the 1857 'Mutiny' and was already working on *The Life of Mahomet* at the time.

It is impossible to separate Muir the scholar from Muir the intelligence officer who witnessed the events of 1857. If the

spectre of 1857 is at least one of the components behind Muir's comments on Islam, it
is, even more significantly, a crucial component in the reaction to *The Life of Mahomet*
among Indian Muslims. There were no million mutinies: the Mutiny had been fought
and lost. The Mughal emperor was a
prisoner of the British, his sons had been
executed, the East India Company had
been replaced by the Crown and the British
were viewing their Muslim subjects with
such suspicion that 13 years after the
Mutiny, despite no further signs of rebellion, 'Governor-General Mayo commissioned W W Hunter to investigate whether
the followers of Islam were obliged to rebel
against the queen.'[6] He needn't have wor-
ried. Although there were cries of 'jihad'
during 1857, the landscape shifted dramat-
ically afterwards:

> [T]he intellectual discourse on *jihad*
> after 1857 was dominated by Indian

> Muslims advocating accommodation
> with colonial rule. Their pragmatic re-
> sponse to British temporal sovereignty
> in India was aimed at securing better
> safeguards for the defeated and demor-
> alised Muslim community.[7]

There was nothing surprising in this:

> [A]n over simplified conception of the
> relation between religion and politics in
> Islam obscures the myriad ways in
> which Muslims [have always] divorced
> faith from politics for tactical and prag-
> matic reasons.[8]

In short, however much offence was in
the air, and there were very good reasons
for not allowing it to spill out in any form
hat might be considered treasonous.

A WAR OF WORDS

Chief among the Muslim pragmatists was
Syed Ahmad Khan, later knighted by the

Crown, who wrote at length about why jihad
was not applicable in the case of British
rule. He used his Urdu translation of, and
commentary on, the Quran as one of several fora for expanding on this view. Briefly,
jihad as aggressive war was only justified
when Muslims were being oppressed specifically because of their religion. Any other
form of suppression was not cause for jihad.
But while making the case for the importance of Muslim loyalty to the British, Sir
Syed was also prepared to turn around and
attack those who attacked Islam. Incensed by
Muir's *Life of Mahomet*, which caused 'an up-
roar in Muslim circles', he wrote 12 essays in
rebuttal in Urdu, which he then had trans-
lated into English as *Essays on the Life of Mo-
hammed*. Other noted scholars, Syed Ameer
Ali (1849–1928) and Maulvi Chiragh Ali
(1844–95), also produced works about the
life of Muhammad designed to defend Islam
against non-Muslim detractors. In using

words to attack those who attacked Islam,
they were drawing on a saying in the Hadith: 'the ink of a scholar is better than the
blood of a martyr.' Those who, in 1857, had
urged their co-religionists to shed martyrs'
blood were not a visible part of the Muir
controversy. Their political moment would
not come again for a long time.

But though 1857 may have ensured that
the hardliners with their appeal to the sword
gave way publicly to the 'good subjects who
were also good Muslims' such as Sir Syed,
the frustrations Sir Syed was to express in
the course of his lifetime regarding the unwillingness of many Indian Muslims to embrace his project to spread education in
subjects such as English and science, without
which he believed progress was impossible,
points to the crisis within Muslim India, a
crisis expressed by the triumph of a 'retreat
and lick wounds' attitude over the 'educate,
educate, educate' attitude of Sir Syed.

There was another crisis playing out at the same time. Sir Syed had originally envisioned himself as an educator concerned with both Hindus and Muslims but after the Hindi–Urdu language controversy in 1867, when Hindus in the United Provinces (renamed Uttar Pradesh post-Independence) demanded that Hindi replace Urdu as an 'official language', he came to view Hindus as intent on erasing Muslim culture and restricted his educational work to the Muslim community. The language controversy led to a war of words between the elites of the Hindu and Muslim communities of North India. The pro-Hindi movement was not widespread among Hindus, but confined to upper-caste North Indian Hindus pushing for the use of Devanagari, a brahmanical writing system. Nevertheless, testifying before an education commission, Ahmad declared that 'Urdu was the language of gentry and Hindi that of the vulgar.'[9] In response, the poet Bharatendu Harishchandra declared: 'There is a secret motive which induces the worshippers of Urdu to devote themselves to its cause. It is the language of dancing girls and prostitutes.'[10]

Muir's comments on Islam were a minor issue compared to the tensions that arose at the upper end of the social strata over the language issue. This had culture and its underlying power tussle, rather than religion, at its heart. Were offences against Urdu a greater crime in the eyes of Muslims than offences against the Prophet? Again, the landscape of Offence can only be understood by considering the politics of the post-1857 moment: the British were the supreme power and there was nothing to be gained by calls to attack them however much their own officials might denigrate Islam. But there was a battle still to be engaged over the position of the different communities of India, more specifically, over the positions of the elites of the different communities of India, and Hindu–Muslim tensions continued to fester, with much assistance from the British and their divide-and-rule policy At the lower end of the social ladder, Hindus and Muslims were equally powerless; both were ignored by their so-called leaders.

All of which is, of course, preamble to the birth of Pakistan, but a necessary preamble given what it reveals about how political considerations guided reactions to offence among the Muslims of South Asia, particularly in the person of Sir Syed, who is a hugely important figure in Pakistan's re-telling of its pre-1947 history.

In the middle of the twentieth century, as British rule ended, intra- and inter-religious tensions and divisions manifested themselves in the events surrounding Partition in 1947. Much has been written about the latter, but there is less discussion

about the religious divisions within India's
Muslim community though this is crucial to
the discussion of the changes in fortune and
political manoeuvring of the hardliners.

Specifically, talk of Pakistan's creation
being based on Islamic ideology, rather
than a claim to Muslim nationhood, side-
steps the fact—inconvenient for Pakistan's
religious establishment and for those who
dismiss it as a nation with a theocratic foun-
dation—that 'the Pakistan movement was
vigorously opposed by virtually the entire
Muslim religious establishment in India'.[11]
Of course, the 'Muslim establishment' was
not itself a unified entity: its components
ranged from the Majlis-e-Ihrar, who regarded the Western-educated leaders of the
pro-Pakistan Muslim League as imperial
stooges, to the Jamaat-e-Islami (JI), who believed that the mere idea of a nation-state
was antithetical to their pan-Islamic vision.
For the latter, the creation of Pakistan was

itself viewed as an Offence to Islam. But once Pakistan became an inevitability, the JI, led by Maulana Maududi, entirely changed its position and tried to find a way to extend its influence in this new nation state, which, Maudidi now declared, had been created solely in order to establish a true Islamic State.

In the early days, the JI had almost no role or influence in the new state. While Mohammad Ali Jinnah's Muslim League was quite happy in its campaign for Pakistan to erase the boundaries between an endangered community (Muslims) and an endangered religion (Islam), the words 'theocratic state' were only uttered in opposition to the notion of Pakistan: 'What are we fighting for? What are we aiming at? It is not theocracy, not for a theocratic state,' Jinnah said in 1946.[12] And on 11 August 1947, in his first speech to the Constituent Assembly, he made one of his most famous declarations, as far from the JI's position as was conceivable:

> You are free; you are free to go to your temples, you are free to go to your mosques or to any other place of worship in this State of Pakistan. You may belong to any religion or caste or creed; that has nothing to do with the business of the State.[13]

CREATING THE NATIONAL MYTH

But if religion had nothing to do with the business of the state, what was the point of Pakistan? The answer returns to that notion, often invoked in the run up to Partition, of Indian Muslims as a distinct minority group and Pakistan as a nation that would ensure that a sizeable—though not majority—part of that minority no longer felt their position, economic, political or cultural, threatened by the majority. But once that nation was achieved, and the majority community was no longer a factor, some other glue had to be found to hold the nation together—some other national myth was necessary.

There is much debate on the reasons for Partition, with widely differing views both within and between the borders of India, Pakistan and Bangladesh. For our purposes here, I mean merely to suggest that Jinnah's speech pointed the way to one possible national myth, that of a nation created to safeguard minorities that would continue to do so: a nation that respected the rights of its different communities. The bloodiness of Partition, the communal violence that accompanied the birth of the nation, could have become the cautionary tale: this is what happens when communities are divided and threatened. Never again, not here, not in our nation.

With Partition violence continuing through the first months of Pakistan's existence, and Hindus being forced from their

homes, could such a myth ever have gained
any ground? And more significantly, was
there a national will to go along with such a
myth, particularly given the 'Islam in Dan-
ger' slogans widely utilized by the Muslim
League in the run up to Partition which
clearly demonstrate that, regardless of the
secular personal nature of the League leadership, the rhetoric it used to win over supporters was not merely about a minority
community but also about the religion itself? We'll never know. No one really made
the attempt to push forward such a myth
and the 'what if' question: 'What if Jinnah
hadn't been a dying man, whose life barely
extended a year into Pakistan's creation?'
must go unanswered.

Instead of the construction of a new national myth based on ideas of community
rights, or indeed any kind of rights, the
first days of Pakistan saw a disintegration of
the often uneasy alliances that had formed

under the banner of Muslim nationhood to counter the perceived threat of a Muslim-unfriendly Hindu majority government:

> Overnight the 'Muslim' identity, behind which disparate forces had all rallied together in the Pakistan movement, was laid aside by the regional groups and new ethnic identities were affirmed.[14]

Pakistan was a nation of five provinces, known at the time as West Punjab, East Bengal, Sindh, Baluchistan and the North West Frontier; it also had a 'new' group, the *muhajirs*, who had migrated across the border at Partition and were largely from the United Provinces. The question of how power would be distributed among the provinces and the ethnicities that composed them quickly became a pressing political issue, in part because, from the outset, the bureaucracy and army were composed largely of Punjabis and, in the early days, in the case of the bureaucracy, *muhajirs*. Other ethnicities, including the Bengalis, who were numerically a majority in the new nation, were vastly under-represented.

In response to demands for a more equitable regional/ethnic power balance, the establishment raised 'a new slogan of the indivisibility of the Muslim Nation':

> A person could not legitimately declare himself or herself to be Bengali or Sindhi or Pathan or Baluch, because he or she was a Muslim, and Islam was a religion of equality and brotherhood and would recognise no divisions amongst the people of the faith.[15]

And so, by 1949, Islamic ideology was trotted out as a politically expedient tool with which to undercut provincial dissent. Nor was provincialism the sole reason for keeping Islam in play: the border dispute with India was also crucial.

Notwithstanding its use of Islamic rhetoric, in the early years the establishment

continued to distance itself clearly from the
religious parties. By 1953, politically marginalized and aware that any 'Islamic provi-
sions' in the Constitution were merely
cosmetic, different groups within the ortho-
doxy banded together at the All-Pakistan-
Muslim-Parties Convention and turned their
attention to the Ahmadi community as a way
of raising their profile and establishing their
credentials as the guardians of Islam.
Though some of their beliefs were considered antithetical to Islam by members of
other sects, the Ahmadis had always defined
themselves as a sect within Islam. Despite
their relatively small number—they were less
than five per cent of the population—the
Ahmadis were economically very successful,
a dangerous combination of vulnerability
and cause for envy.

The APMC demanded that members of
the Ahmadi sect be declared non-Muslim
and all Ahmadis, including the current for-

eign minister, be removed from government positions. Despite the political embarrassment of seeing members of its own party giving implicit support to this proposal as a way of boosting their own popularity, the government refused the demands. The APMC paraded this as an Offence against Islam, a failure to live up to Islamic values, and carefully orchestrated riots which ushered in Pakistan's first bout of Martial Law. The riots were put down, a trial commenced and, for his part in the anti-Ahmadi riots, Maududi was sentenced to death. The sentence was later commuted and he was released from prison in 1955.

The extensive Munir–Kayani Report, which was commissioned to look into the causes of the riots, is a remarkable document, not least for its insights into the dangers of mixing religion and politics, and the quagmire of defining who is and is not Muslim. To establish this, the writers of the

Report asked nine leading figures of the *ulema* (religious scholars) to define 'the irreducible minimum conditions which a person must satisfy to be entitled to be called a Muslim'. The widely varying responses lead the authors to observe dryly:

> Need we make any comment except that no two learned divines are agreed on this fundamental. If we attempt our own definition as each learned divine has done and that definition differs from that given by all others, we unanimously go out of the fold of Islam. And if we adopt the definition given by any one of the *ulama*, we remain Muslims according to the view of that *alim* but *kafirs* according to the definition of every one else.[16]

The religious parties may have learned from this episode the extent of damage they could do to the functioning of the state via street power inflamed by religious rhetoric, but they would also have learned that the government could, in turn, take severe action against the hardliners. For the next few years, the hardliners were fairly quiet.

The rise of the Left in the 1960s shifted the oppositional position of the JI and the establishment by providing them with a common enemy; the JI's student wing became notorious for its violent suppressions of leftist movements on campus and gained the support of a state that saw populist movements as the real threat to its power. Despite the strong role of religion in the personal lives of most Pakistanis, and despite the JI's continuing claims to be the only true guardians of Islam, it was by no means a populist party. Though it did have a significant power base on university campuses where the fiery rhetoric of its leaders won much favour with Pakistan's disaffected youth, it was unlikely to threaten the establishment.

The JI's inability to widen its support base was brought home in the 1970 general election, Pakistan's first in the 33 years since Independence. In East Pakistan, Mujib-ur-Rehman's Awami League won a landslide victory and was the overall victor across the two wings of the country. In West Pakistan, the winner was Zulfiqar Ali Bhutto's Pakistan Peoples Party (PPP). Bengali nationalism on one hand and promises of social justice on the other were the real charges that ignited Pakistan's voters. The religious parties were routed: of the 300 seats in the National Assembly, the three main religious parties only won 19 between them—a trend that was repeated in all but one of the general elections that were to follow in the next 38 years. However, the Jamiat-Ulema Islami (JUI), a long dormant party, which had seen its fortune revive during the popular agitation against Ayub Khan's military regime in the 1960s, now

joined the JI as a highly visible player on
the political scene

The failure of both the establishment
and Bhutto to accept the result of the elections and allow Mujib to take his place as
Prime Minister led to civil war and the creation of Bangladesh. Earlier, provincial differences had led to assertions of 'Muslim
nationhood' in an attempt to stem demands
for greater provincial autonomy; now, the
anti-Bengali sentiment necessary to back
the violent suppression of the Bengali na-
tionalists was stoked by claims that Bengali
Muslims were 'tainted by Hinduism'. Any
group or organization that really cared
about Offence to Islam would have raised
its voice in horror at the Muslim-on-Muslim
rape and murder the army carried out in
East Pakistan, but such voices were shamefully absent. Provincial chauvinism, vested
economic interests, considerations of political power, continuing conflicts with India

that perpetuated the India=Hindu=enemy rhetoric of the Partition era—all these were stronger than any Islamic values of brotherhood or unity. The insistence that the majority of Muslims necessarily view each other as part of an extended *ummah* and consider an offence to one as an offence to all entirely ignores the bloodiness of intra-religious encounters between Muslims throughout history. For Pakistanis, 1971 in particular stands between any claim to concern for the *ummah*.

MILITANT SECULARISM

Zulfiqar Ali Bhutto, whose premiership lasted from 1971 to 1977, was voted into power in West Pakistan—Pakistan, as it had now become—on the basis of his socialist '*roti, kapra, makaan*' (food, clothing and shelter) agenda. In Tariq Ali's analysis:

> He was the only political leader Pakistan has ever produced who had the power,

buttressed by mass support, to change the country and its institutions, including the army, for ever. But he failed on every front.[17]

As opposition to Bhutto grew, so did the prominence of the religious parties, which were among the most vociferous of anti-Bhutto voices. By 1974, those voices seemed to be shouting from all directions. The two most politically marginalized of Pakistan's provinces—Baluchistan and the North West Frontier Province—were both in a state of insurrection after Bhutto's dismissal of their provincial governments on the grounds that they were engaged in anti-state activity; 19 members of the military were found guilty of conspiring against Bhutto by a court-martial; within the PPP, the growing power of land-owners was causing considerable dissent from the more left-leaning 'old guard'.

Faced by a host of problems on the national front, Bhutto was seeking to extend his influence as a regional leader. In the wake of the 1973 oil crisis, he recognized the oil-producing Arab nations as major power players to whom he wanted to ally himself; his hosting of the Second Islamic Summit was the most visible sign of this. But this new regional association meant allying himself with Saudi Arabia and its ultra-hardline, puritanical Wahabi version of Islam, closely tied to Maududi's JI. It is against the background of both the growing opposition clamour within Pakistan and Bhutto's aspirations for regional leadership that we must consider the re-awakening of the anti-Ahmadi movement. Once more, the JI was at the forefront of the movement to declare Ahmadis non-Muslim and Bhutto a 'bad Muslim' for his support to that community, many of whose members had backed him in the 1970 elections. But Bhutto saw an opportunity not only to discredit the JI's claims and ease the opposition pressure, but also to win points with

Saudi Arabia, who, in April that year, had
hosted a World Muslim League Conference
at which it called on all Muslims countries
to declare the Ahmadis non-Muslim:
Bhutto's government passed a resolution
declaring the Ahmadis non-Muslim.

This was a defining moment in the history of Islam and Offence in Pakistan. In
Jalal's view, it may be the single most significant moment in the relationship of state
and religion:

> The Ahmadi controversy showed how
> pressure politics clothed in Islamic rhet-
> oric could be applied in Pakistan . . .
> Pakistan after 1974 was up for grabs for
> anyone who could muster the street
> power to pronounce any Pakistani a
> non-Muslim.[18]

Rather than giving the religious parties
any reason to back down, Bhutto's move
against the Ahmadis became encouragement
for further demands in the name of Islam.

By 1977, nine opposition parties in Pakistan had banded together as the Pakistan National Alliance (PNA). The groups comprising the PNA had varying political and ideological stances and were united only by their anti-Bhutto agenda. Yet, despite their differences and despite the presence of secular politicians in the PNA, 'Islam' became their rallying cry.

Part of the PNA's anti-Bhutto campaign focused on his 'un-Islamic' consumption of alcohol. In response to this, Bhutto declared at a large public rally: 'They say I drink. Yes, I drink. I drink alcohol, but at least I don't drink the people's blood.' This dig at his opponents was greeted with sustained roars of approval from the crowd. But though Bhutto had correctly anticipated his supporters' lack of appetite for 'Islamic values', within a few months he had changed his stance: as at the time of the Ahmadi question, he decided to try and outmanoeuvre his opponents by taking on the mantle of Islam himself. He banned alcohol and gambling, and declared Friday a public holiday in place of Sunday. Rather than outflanking the religious parties, however, this merely moved the nation further in an Islamist direction.

And it did nothing for Bhutto's political career either. Within weeks, the army, headed by Zia-ul-Haq, was in power and Bhutto was in prison. He was hanged two years later, by which point Zia was firmly set on the path of introducing hardline Islam into the constitution and character of the nation.

MILITARY ISLAM

Prior to Zia, Pakistan's leaders had often raised the banner of Islam as a politically expedient tool, but, apart from Bhutto's banning of the Ahmadis for reasons both political and personal, they had always ensured that Islam remained at best a cosmetic gloss to the functioning of the state. With Zia, that old order was to be turned firmly on its head.

From the start, Zia allied himself with the JI, which was finally in a position to bring about the 'Islamization' of the country. All other political leaders were in prison or in exile, and censorship was firmly in place. Into this political vacuum Zia introduced the infamous 'Hudood Ordinances'. Though these were ostensibly Islamic Laws, it is notable that in his quest for a truly Islamic state Zia did not touch the economic functioning of the nation and only concentrated on 'social' aspects. The Munir–Kayani Report of 1954 may have demonstrated that Islamic laws could not be constitutionally enshrined since there was such a wide body of opinion regarding even the most basic tenants of Islam, but all that was now swept aside and Zia's Islam became Pakistan's Islam.

And what did Zia's Islam consist of? Lashing, amputation, stoning to death—all in public. Most offensive of all to Muslims for whom theirs was a religion of justice, the Hudood Ordinances allowed for rape victims to be tried for adultery and stoned to death. This was, of course, a law that primarily targeted women, a group whom Zia's Islamization was particularly concerned with. By the next year, female spectator sports were banned and female government employees and female models on television were all required to observe Islamic dress codes. All this was not sufficient for Zia's Islam. In 1983, the Islamic Law of Evidence decreed that in legal matters the evidence of two women is equal to that of one man; the evidence of a sole woman was not admitted. In the same year, the government-appointed Ansari Commission recommended that women be barred from high political office and any woman contesting elections for 'lower' office should have written permission from her husband. This was also the year that, under the Hudood Ordinances, Safia Bibi, a blind 13-year-old girl who was raped but couldn't identify her attackers, was found guilty of adultery and sentenced to imprisonment, a fine and a public lashing.

Zia must have thought that in his legal and constitutional assaults on women he was taking on a group that, in a highly patriarchal country, had little voice or power. But the Women's Action Forum (WAF), a women's rights organization, which had formed in response to the Hudood Ordinances, had other ideas. Though WAF was formed as early as 1981, it was really in 1983 that it fully entered national consciousness with a demonstration in Lahore against the Law of Evidence, which saw

hundreds of women protestors assaulted by
the police. WAF's protest marches, signa-
ture campaigns and other forms of pressure
tactics forced Zia's government onto the
back-foot for the first time since 1977. In
1983 alone, the Law of Evidence was
amended and Safia Bibi was acquitted. The
Ansari Commission's recommendations
never became law.

No discussion of Islam and Offence in
Pakistan can ignore the immense importance of the women's movement in the Zia
years. While politicians have a long history
of unwillingness to take the hardliners on
headfirst for fear of alienating segments of
a populace who might view such an attack
as directed against Islam itself, the women's
movement showed how it was possible to
launch such an attack by revealing the
hypocrisy at the core of so-called Islamization and raising the right to question interpretations of Islam. It was not Islam itself,

but those purporting to be its guardians whom WAF identified as the guilty party. This form of criticism entered the cultural sphere through feminist poets who were an important part of the women's movement.

Poets have had a long and distinguished tradition of political activism as well as being significant players in anti-authoritarian movements. The wide appeal of poetry in Pakistan makes them a particular target for repressive governments. One of the most notable of the poet-activists during Zia's regime was Fehmida Riaz whose long poem 'Will You Not See the Full Moon' savages the government with its clear argument that 'Islamization is simply a ruse with which the rulers defuse dissent and construct consent while dividing the nation sharply between those who have economic and political power and those who do not.'[19] The poem ends with a swipe at Pakistan's growing dependence on Saudi Arabia:

We are grinding humans to produce
    dwarves
O Sheikh, praise our achievements!
Alms! O Brother!
I swear by your hallowed petrodollars.[20]

For her outspoken views, Riaz was forced into exile by Zia's government.

The word 'petrodollars'—in English in the original poem—also gestures towards that other increasingly important nation with which Zia's government was politically and financially enmeshed: the USA.

The US and Pakistan had been allies from the start, though the relationship turned frosty in Bhutto's days when his plans to start a nuclear programme met with strong warnings of aid withdrawal from Henry Kissinger. In response, Bhutto declared his bomb an 'Islamic bomb' as a way of appealing to the oil-rich Arab nations for financial assistance to cover the threatened loss of US aid. It was not during Bhutto's premiership, however, but during the very first months of Zia's rule that the US cut off economic and military aid to Pakistan in response to its continued nuclear programme.

But the Soviet invasion of Afghanistan in 1979 pushed all considerations of Pakistan's nuclear programme to one side. For the next nine years, Pakistan was the US's most necessary ally in the cold war and, as the conduit through which arms and finances passed into the hands of the mujahideen (anti-Soviet resistance fighters in Afghanistan), Zia's government was also in a position to decide which groups to favour and which to marginalize. Unsurprisingly, he chose to favour the most hardline Islamist groups, not only because they reflected his ideological bent but also because he wanted to ensure an Afghanistan of the future that would be Pakistan-friendly rather than India-friendly.

The Afghan War brought 'the Kalashnikov culture' to Pakistan as the country became 'the world's largest open market in arms'.[21] From here on, anyone with a grudge to settle or a point to make would also have a weapon. It altered the entire social fabric of the nation. But it wasn't enough merely to arm the Afghan mujahideen. In Ahmad's words:

> In an effort to mobilise the entire Muslim world against the 'evil empire', the CIA started supporting the flow of volunteers from all around the world to fight in Afghanistan . . . Militants were recruited and flown in. I have seen planeloads of them arriving from Algeria, Sudan, Saudi Arabia, Egypt, Jordan, even from Palestine . . . These people were brought in, given an ideology and told armed struggle is virtuous.[22]

This jihadi recruitment took strong root in Pakistan as well, of course. To Zia and his increasingly powerful and reactionary Inter Services Intelligence (ISI) agency, jihad was a useful tool, not merely in Afghanistan but also in Kashmir, which continued to be a matter of some obsession for the Pakistan army. What the jihadis could achieve in Afghanistan against the might of the Soviet Union, Zia's men reasoned, they could also achieve in Kashmir against the lesser might of India.

Nationally, regionally, globally, hardline Islam was in the ascendant and was now terrifyingly well armed and well connected through its close political affiliation with the country that was soon to be the world's only superpower. Pakistan, meanwhile, was flush with military and financial aid, as with new mosques and madrasas (religious schools), often funded by the Saudis and run by the hardliners allied to Zia. A new generation of Pakistanis was growing up in a world in which the tentacles of Zia's Islam were everywhere.

Although the mystical Sufi tradition continued to be the dominant expression of Islam in many parts of the country—particularly in Sindh and Punjab—something essential had shifted in the relationship of the nation and religion. Sara Suleri talks about the beginning of this shift in her memoir *Meatless Days* (1991), dating it to the Bhutto days:

> I think we dimly knew we were about to witness Islam's departure from the land of Pakistan. The men would take it to the streets and make it vociferate, but the great romance between religion and the populace, the embrace that engendered Pakistan, was done . . . God could now leave the home and soon would join the government.[23]

By the end of the Zia years, religion was firmly wrapped up in government, and belief became something increasingly represented outwardly: in clothing, in facial hair, in marks on the forehead denoting prostration during prayertime. Internal, intimate belief was no longer the order of the day.

Pakistan had 11 years of Zia's rule, 11 years of increased radicalization. At the end of it all, just months after the Soviets withdrew from Afghanistan, Zia was killed by a bomb and Pakistan's populace voted into power a woman opposed by all the religious parties. Economic concerns, provincial concerns, pro-democracy concerns, cynicism about the *maulvis* (an honorific prefix given to Muslim scholars) were all still much stronger than any desire for further 'Islamization'. Yet the fact that the woman in question, Benazir Bhutto, had taken to covering her head, a public image quite different from the one in sleeveless blouses and saris to which the nation had become accustomed during her father's time in office, showed just how much the political landscape had shifted towards 'outward observance'.

All the same, the religious parties fared
badly in the 1988 elections: the JUI only
managed seven seats out of the 207 in the
National Assembly and though the JI was
part of the coalition of nine parties that
won 54 seats, most of those went to the
Nawaz Sharif-led Pakistan Muslim League
(PML). Yet the JI was still a senior player in
the opposition, and the PML, which was
closely tied to the old Zia regime, was more
than slightly sympathetic to their politics.
More than that, the name chosen by the
coalition, the Islamic Democratic Alliance,
pointed to their willingness to claim the title
of Islam's guardians against the new Western-educated female head of state. The Alliance also had two crucial supporters in the
all-powerful ISI and the army, who saw no
reason why the will of the people should in-
terfere with their strategic objectives for the
region.

In other words, there were powerful factions that wanted to see the Bhutto government fall. All they needed was an opportunity to destabilize her government. And then came *The Satanic Verses*.

On 12 February 1989, thousands of demonstrators took part in a protest rally against *The Satanic Verses* at the American Cultural Centre in Islamabad. The protest was lead by prominent 'religious leaders' who had long ago learned the value of street power as opposed to popular political support. The demonstrators threw stones, the police responded first with tear gas then bullets. Five of the protestors were killed. Benazir Bhutto, just over two months into her first term of office, was under no doubt as to the motives behind the protest:

> The question that perturbs the present
> Government was whether the agitation
> was really against the book, which has

not been read in Pakistan, is not for
sale in Pakistan and has not been trans-
lated in Pakistan . . . Or was it a protest
by those who lost the election, or those
who were patronised by martial law to
try and destabilise the process of
democracy?[24]

There were, of course, those who in-
sisted there were no underlying political
motives, but the choice of protest venue
certainly seemed to suggest otherwise. The
author of the book was not American; the
original publishers of the book were not
American. Why then target the American
Cultural Centre? Could it have had something to do with the events of the preceding
year? This was a year in which the Pak-
American alliance in Afghanistan had com-
pletely disintegrated and the US showed it
couldn't leave the region fast enough, while
Pakistan felt there was much work left to be
done in order to install a Pak-friendly government in Afghanistan. In Pakistan, wide-

spread opinion, cutting across the political spectrum, was that the US had deserted Pakistan. Any protest rally that could combine anti-Americanism with a defence of Islam was inevitably going to hit a nerve.

All of which explains why, at 16, I couldn't understand why boys were burning books in Bradford.

As had her father before her, Benazir Bhutto chose to try to accommodate the religious parties rather than take them on. Perhaps no group felt more betrayed than sections of the women's movement. They had been her staunch supporters yet saw her elected into office twice without making any move to repeal the Hudood Ordinances, or even to open discussion on the matter. Those more sympathetic to Bhutto argued that it would be political suicide for a woman to take on the religious right, which in a post-Zia world had more supporters in the establishment than she did.

In the 11 years after Zia died, the democratic politicians either played along with the religious parties—as in the case of Nawaz Sharif, whose government extended the Blasphemy Laws which have been repeatedly used to persecute Pakistan's Hindus and Christians—or tried to accommodate them—as did Benazir Bhutto. This goes far to explain the otherwise perplexing support that some of the most socially liberal segments of society offered General Pervez Musharraf when he came to power in a military coup in 1999. Musharraf's first interview as head of state showed pictures of him cuddling his pet dogs—considered 'unclean' by the hardliners—and talking about his great admiration for the Turkish secularist leader Kemal Ataturk. Both were seen as signs of his willingness to take on the religious extremists whose influence had grown in the decade since the Taliban had taken power in Afghanistan; the border between the countries was so porous that a Taliban government in Afghanistan had ensured 'Talibanization' took firm root in the Frontier where the pro-Taliban JUI had its support base.

But that one interview was to prove an exception. Musharraf was never again photographed with his dogs and saved his comments on Ataturk for state visits to Turkey. It was clear the President and Chief of Army Staff, a man seemingly with complete power, had been warned against offending members of the only power-base he needed to worry about with his liberal stance towards religion—his own armed forces.

HOW THE USA BECAME THE GREAT OTHER

The Jew as well as the Christian, the Hindu no less than the Muslim 'fundamentalist' plies an ideology of

> superior difference. Each confronts
> an inferior and threatening Other.[25]

Eqbal Ahmad's analysis of religious extremists raises an interesting issue with particular regard to Pakistan.

> The Other is always an active negation. All such movements mobilise hatred and often harness unusual organisational effort to do so.[26]

The Other, who can also be termed The Offensive One, has a deeply entrenched position in Pakistan's history. I'm referring, of course, to India.

The dispute over Kashmir, which started at the moment of Pakistan's inception, ensured that the anti-Hindu rhetoric that had been such a part of the Pakistan Movement never became a thing of the past. Never mind the large Muslim population in India, India was equated with Hindus who were equated with the enemies of Islam/Pakistan. This is a key factor in the role of religion in Pakistan and one of the reasons behind the fluttering of the banner of Islam. For unpopular governments, India has always been a convenient way of distracting attention from the nation's internal problems. But precisely because the anti-India rhetoric was so widespread and so institutionalized, there was not much to be gained for the religious parties from agitational politics around the subject of Hindus, which may explain why they turned their attention to the Ahmadis.

But with the Ahmadis marginalized, the religious groups clearly needed Another Other, one against whom they could firmly define themselves to prove their Guardians of Islam credentials. It was as early as November 1979 that the US was identified as the Other Other, when a group of JI students, inflamed by rumours that the US and Israel were behind attacks on the Great Mosque in Medina, attacked the US Embassy in Islamabad. But within weeks of this attack the Soviets invaded Afghanistan and the close embrace between Zia's government, backed by the JI, and the US meant it wasn't politically expedient to continue this line of agitation. That changed once the US withdrew its support for Pakistan's Afghan policy when the Soviet Union withdrew at the end of the 1980s.

Anti-Americanism was, and continues to be a rich vein to be mined in the Pakistani psyche. When the great alliance between Pakistan and the US, which continued through Zia's years of oppressing his own citizens, came to an end with the withdrawal of the Soviets, the US rediscovered its objections, dormant through the 1980s, to Pakistan's nuclear programme and imposed economic sanctions in 1990. That most Pakistanis viewed a nuclear programme as a necessary defensive response to India's nuclear programme didn't help with the sentiment towards the US.

As long as the Other was India, it was difficult to generate rhetorical steam from events unfolding outside the region. Zulfiqar Bhutto tried hard to make Kashmir a 'Muslim issue', declaring Pakistan's support for the Palestinians in the hope of receiving reciprocal support from the Arab nations over Kashmir. But it was in no one's strategic interest other than Pakistan's to make India a key concern. India as the enemy of Islam was a position that had few takers outside Pakistan, and it was hard to make the case that India was oppressing the pan-Islamic world.

But the US was another matter entirely. With its strategic interest in the oil-producing nations—and, after 2001, Afghanistan again—the US and its NATO allies were soon generating barrels of polemic for the Muslim radicals in need of an Other. Now it was strategically valuable for radicals from different parts of the world, many with

overlapping histories of failed postcolonial
states, to make common cause, find a common enemy and declare that an attack on a
Muslim by the US and its NATO allies was
an attack on all Muslims. The identification
of this common enemy and common cause,
which is discussed in various terms—the
US, the West, the Secular World, the Unbelievers—made it easy to create the impres-
sion that Muslims around the world were
banding together and closing ranks. Yet
throughout this time, Muslims continued to
kill Muslims, Shia and Sunni continued to
declare each other Unbelievers, backdoor
conversations went on between Muslims
who declared themselves allies of the US
and Muslims who declared themselves enemies of the US. Political power and material
possessions proved stronger than religious
fellow-feeling and moderates and extremists continued to battle it out in print, in
political campaigns, in opposing fatwas

from mosques within a few square miles of
each other and so on.

The First Gulf War saw the great up-
surge of anti-US rhetoric but it was the war
in Afghanistan in 2001 that saw the rhetoric
reach a peak in Pakistan. What the US tried
to sell as 'War on Terror', Pakistanis saw as a
war on Afghans. More specifically, the Pashtuns of the Frontier Province saw it as a war
on Pashtuns. The Durand Line, which divided Pakistani Pashtuns from Afghan Pashtuns, had always been viewed as entirely
artificial by the Pashtuns themselves. Now
they saw their 'brothers', earlier 'deserted'
by the US, being attacked in response to the
actions of 18 Saudis and one Turk. Many
continued to believe the accused couldn't
possibly have been behind the attacks because, as I heard more than once, 'No Arab
could pull off something like that.' The
racism between Muslim nations is acute.
And worst of all, the Pakistan government

was the US's frontline ally in this attack. Small wonder then that the 2002 election became the only general election in Pakistan's history that saw the religious parties, now allied in a single coalition, the Muttahida Majlis-e-Amal (MMA), win significant gains and emerge as the third largest party in parliament, taking control of the two provinces bordering Afghanistan. It was anti-Americanism rather than promises of Islamization that the MMA played up most strongly in its electioneering.

It is notable that the US invasion of Afghanistan didn't cause the kind of outcry in other Muslim nations that it did in Pakistan and Afghanistan. It would take the invasion of Iraq for the countries of the Middle East to get truly worked up.

But there was another narrative working its way through all this, adding its poison to the blood stream: Islam vs Christendom or Islam vs the West. It had never really gone away. There was a brief flickering moment at the time of Independence when it seemed the trajectory that started when the East India Company began to gain political ascendancy in the 1700s might be reversed. The British had been sent packing; a Muslim nation had emerged. But that nation quickly became a US client state. The trajectory was continuing. Musharraf's readiness to join the attack on Afghanistan came to be seen as a pointed reminder of this client-state status. Much of the rage generated by the US and its Western allies comes from the stark reminder of this trajectory of failure that is reflected both in the particular case of Pakistan and in the wider case of many Muslim nations.

And yet, Islam and those who offend it are far from being the chief concern of most of Pakistan's populace. Economics remains the most crucial issue in a nation with shamefully high poverty rates. Provin-

cial ties outstrip claims to shared Muslimness. And there's a healthy level of scepti-
cism around the so-called Guardians of
Islam. The most recent election results in
2008 amply demonstrated this: the religious parties, who had come to power in
2002 on a wave of anti-Americanism, were
all shunted out again and, in the two
provinces they governed, the music they
had banned rang out in celebration.

It is galling, then, for the nation to see
itself viewed as almost entirely composed of
religious fanatics—particularly when the
well-armed and well-funded religious fanatics are targeting and oppressing large segments of the population. The notion that
the West is perpetuating images of violence
and extremism among Muslims—and
downplaying all evidence of moderate
Islam—in order to gain support for attacks
on Islam and Muslims finds voice throughout Pakistan.

kamila shamsie

In closing, it's worth looking at the
most recent incident in which the transnational figure of the Offended Muslim reap-
peared in blood and fire: the Danish
Cartoon Controversy. In much of Europe
and the US, the prevailing notion is that
the publication of the cartoons led to an in-
stant reaction from Muslims across the
globe who resorted to violence and death
threats. But, in Pakistan, the immediate reaction was of a different sort. Yes, people
were offended. Deeply so. Nothing written
in this essay should undermine how
strongly most Pakistani Muslims feel about
attacks on the Prophet. But in terms of public responses, here's what happened.[27] The
Pakistan foreign office said the cartoons
'encourage sinister agendas for the clash of
civilisations'; an All-Parties-Conference was
called by members of various political
groups to launch a movement against 'the
planned conspiracy by the West to instigate

73

the Muslims'; the head of the pro-Taliban
JUI, now Chief Minister in the Frontier
Provinces, said the cartoons were aimed at
sparking 'the clash of civilizations'.

In other words, across the political
spectrum there was scant support for the
notion that such a clash was either in-
evitable or ongoing; but there was a concern, sometimes tipping into paranoia, that
a great many people outside the Muslim
world wished to see that imagined incom-
patibility in worldviews become reality. Of
course, the comments on 'clash of civilizations' didn't get picked up by anyone other
than the Pakistani press. But, a few days
later, there was a protest in Lahore that
turned violent and led to the deaths of two
people. With the main religious parties now
in government, it's worth noting that the
call for the protest didn't come from either
the JI or the JUI but from a group of small
parties who banded together and coordi-

nated the protest with many local madrasas.
The value of street power, the ease with
which violence can be started and spread—
these are lessons Pakistan's political parties,
religious and otherwise, have learned well
over the years.

In Pakistan, over the next few days, we
watched as images of the violence in Lahore
played out on media channels across the
world alongside images of protest, flag-
burning, calls for violence from bearded
men in different parts of the world. There
we were, part of the Muslim Monolith, En-
raged and Out of Control.

But why don't those Muslims who aren't
part of the Violently Offended stage their
own protest rallies against those who spread
the image of Islam as a religion of violence,
friends have sometimes asked me. In part,
it's simply because the violence of the hardliners intimidates more pacifist sections of
the population. But that's not the whole

story. It's also true that most practicing
Muslims really are deeply offended by real
or perceived attacks on Islam and so will
not protest against those who set themselves up as Guardians of Islam for concern
that they might appear to be 'siding with'
those who offend Islam. There is too small
a space for those who oppose-attacks-on-
Islam and also oppose-violence-in-the-
name-of-Islam. The feeling that 'the West'
deliberately chooses to insult Islam and
then uses protests against those insults as
an occasion to brand all Muslims 'fanatics'
makes a great many people uneasy about
standing up on the side of 'the West'.

The only way out of this vicious circle of
mutual suspicion is for both sides to take a
closer look at each other. A closer look at
the Muslims of the world reveals many different pieces in the Mosaic of the Offended
Muslim. An even closer look reveals that
the Mosaic of the Offended Muslim is only

a small part of the larger Mosaic of Muslims. But there is no denying that for reasons to do with national and global politics,
with the former being the more significant
component, religious extremism is on the
rise. In Pakistan, there was a time when the
JI was the most extremist of politically significant organizations. Then the JUI came
along and made the former seem moderate
by comparison. But both the JUI and JI
worked towards being part of the political
set-up, with all the compromises and ac-
commodations that politics makes necessary. Since Pakistan's armed forces joined
the 'War on Terror', there has been an increased response from armed militants—
former jihadis who now feel betrayed by the
Pakistan state that once thought it expedient to back them and train them—with no
interest in the political process and whose
sole desire is to extend their writ over sections of Pakistan through capturing terri-

tory rather than votes. They, in turn, have
made the JUI seem centrist by comparison.

There is a deep crisis in Pakistan, its
roots in provincial imbalance and the failure
of the state to provide for its citizens, which
creates a vacuum into which the religious
parties have stepped with their free education in madrasas and other acts of civic re-
sponsibility. After the 2006 earthquake, for
instance, the extremist organization Jamaat-
e Dawa was far more visible than any government agency in helping the wounded
and recovering bodies for burial. In addition, the political manipulation of religion
by all parties and governments through Pakistan's history, the use of jihadism as a tool to
increase regional power, the dependence on
US military and financial aid, which ties national self-interest to US demands, the dependence on Saudi aid, which allows
Wahabism to spread via mosques and
madrasas in regions where Sufism has been

the dominant expression of Islam for centuries, further aggravates the situation. That many of these issues find echoes or overlaps in other Muslim-majority postcolonial states creates an image of sameness across the Muslim world. But it isn't so. To say otherwise would be to allow Pakistan's politicians, its bureaucracy, its religious leaders, its intelligence agencies and its army off the hook for their successive and continuing failures.

Notes

1   William Dalrymple, 'A Bloody Warning to Today's Imperial Occupiers'. *Guardian* (10 May 2007).

2   Eqbal Ahmad, *The Selected Writings* (Columbia: Columbia University Press, 2006), p. 160.

3   Ibid., p. 173.

4   William Muir, *Life of Mahomet*, *Volume 4* (London: Smith, Elder and Company, 1861), p. 321.

5 Ayesha Jalal, *Partisans of Allah*: *Jihad in South Asia* (Cambridge, MA: Harvard University Press, 2008), p. 151.

6 Ibid., p. 136.

7 Ibid., p. 176.

8 Ibid., p. 149.

9 R. Upadhyay, *Urdu Controversy* (India: South Asia Analysis Group, 2003). Available at: www.southasiaanalysis.org/papers 7/paper675.html

10 Sagaree Sengupta, 'Krsna and the Cruel Beloved: Hariscandra and Urdu', *Annual of Urdu Studies 9* (1994): 87.

11 Hamza Alavi, 'Pakistan and Islam: Ethnicity and Ideology', in Fred Halliday and Hamza Alavi (eds) *State and Ideology in the Middle East and Pakistan* (London/New York: Monthly Review Press, 1988). Also avilable at: ourworld.compuserve.com/ homepages/sangat/Pakislam.htm

12 Ahmad, *Selected Writings*, p. 420.

13 *Dawn* (Independence Day Supplement), 14 August 1999. [Transcribed from printed copy by Shehzaad Nakhoda.]

14 Alavi, 'Pakistan and Islam'.

15 Ibid.

16 M. Munir and M. R. Kayani, *Report of the Court of Inquiry Constituted under Punjab Act II of 1954 to Enquire into the Punjab Disturbances of 1953* (Lahore: Printed by the Superintendent, Government Printing, Punjab, 1954), p. 227.

17 Tariq Ali, 'The General in His Labyrinth', *London Review of Books* (4 January 2007).

18 Jalal, *Partisans of Allah*, p. 273.

19 Ali Husain Mir and Raza Mir, *Anthems of Resistance* (New Delhi: India Ink, 2006), p. 221.

20 Ibid., p. 220. Translation by the authors.

21 Eqbal Ahmad, 'Bloody Games', *The New Yorker* (11 April 1988).

22 David Barsamian, *Eqbal Ahmad: Confronting Empire* (Cambridge, MA: South End Press, 2000), p. 91.

23 Sara Suleri, *Meatless Days* (Chicago: University of Chicago Press, 1991), p.15

24 Barbara Crossette, 'Attack on US Site in Pakistan Growing into Crisis for Bhutto',

The New York Times (14 February 1989).

25 Ahmad, *Selected Writings*, p. 187

26 Ibid.

27 Much of the next two paragraphs is taken from 'Agent Provocateur', an op-ed piece I wrote for *The New York Times* (15 February 2006).

INDEX
ON CENSORSHIP

Index on Censorship is Britain's leading organisation promoting freedom of expression. Our award-winning magazine and website provide a window for original, challenging and intelligent writing on this vital issue around the world. Our international projects in media, arts and education put our philosophy into action.

For information and enquiries go to <u>www.indexoncensorship.org</u>, or email enquiries@indexoncensorship.org

To subscribe to *Index on Censorship*, or find stockists in your area, go to http://www.indexoncensorship.org/getyourcopy
or phone
(+44) 20 7017 5544 for the United Kingdom or
(+1) 518 537 4700 in the United States

www.indexoncensorship.org